Skookum's North

The "PAWS" Collection by Doug Urquhart

LOST MOOSE PUBLISHING, WHITEHORSE, YUKON

Published by Lost Moose Publishing, Whitehorse, Yukon, Canada

Canadian Cataloguing in Publication Data

Urquhart, Doug.

    Skookum's North

    ISBN 0-9694612-3-2

    1. Comic books, strips, etc., Canadian (English) * 2. Canada, Northern—Social conditions—Comic books, strips, etc. 3. Skookum (Fictitious character) I. Title. II. Title: PAWS collection.

PN6734.S56U68 1994   741.5'971   C94-910426-4

Printed and bound in Canada

For information on this and other books from Lost Moose Publishing see back of book.

FT. DOGGEREL TRADING POST

Phoebe: *Vic's wife and Rosie's best friend*

Victor Conibear: *Ace trapper and Marten's best friend*

Rosie: *Marten's wife*

Marten Fisher: *Skookum's partner in bush survival*

Winchester: *The Fisher's kid*

Mossbum: *Wheel dog of little brain*

Skookum: *Intrepid lead dog and Marten's best buddy*

Rufus: *Skookum's intellectual sidekick*

Psycho: *The silent one*

Skookum's North

In the far north, somewhere between the tundra and the mountains, is a tiny community called Ft. Doggerel. Located where the Rabid River flows into beautiful Mush Lake, the few hundred inhabitants—and their humans— live as perpetual misfits, drifting back and forth between town life and bush life. Here, these modern northerners try to worship material wealth, comfort, success and safety, like other people, but find themselves unable to resist the beauty, freedom and adventure that beckons from the edge of town. *(After all, they only moved to town in the first place because the government told them they were impoverished, ignorant and uncivilized and had to be properly "administrated.")*

This is Ft. Doggerel. For generations, the families of Skookum the husky dog and his human provider, Marten Fisher, have hung around this spot where Marten's great grandfather built a trading post. According to husky lore, he married a young woman who had a notoriously handsome and fearless lead dog, probably Skookum's ancestor. *(This may have been the original* "Dog-girl," *which some say gave rise to the name* "Doggerel." *Others believe it came from* "Dog-growl." *Scientists love to argue about this, but the locals know it has a more poetic meaning.)*

Today, the people living this unique northern lifestyle are sometimes called "bush rats," other times much worse. But that's because nobody ever really explained how marvellous and rewarding their lives truly are. Until ***"Skookum's North"***…

1983

GEE GEE **GEE!** YOU ✱✵ POTLICKER!

...PLEASE?

SOMETIMES YOU GOTTA BE RUTHLESS IF YOU WANT A GOOD MUSHER!

ZOOM

WHUMP!

I TOLD YOU TO **KEEP OFFA MY** ✱✵✸!!! **SNOWSHOES!**

IS IT MY FAULT THE OTHERS BUNCH UP BEHIND ME? WHY CAN'T YOU TRAIN THEM TO STAY IN LINE?

LET'S FACE IT... A GEORGE ATTLA HE AIN'T!

...(GRUNT)...(OOF!) MARTEN'S MAKING ME GO AND TRAIN VICTOR'S NEW TEAM

THERE'LL BE THE USUAL DOMINANCE FIGHTS, THE TORN EARS, SLASHED LEGS, PUNCTURED NOSES...UNLESS

FT. DOGGEREL

...IT'S AN **ALL GIRL TEAM!**

1

ICE FISHING IS SO BORING

YAHOO! WE GOT A BIG ONE!

ITS TOO BIG FOR THE HOLE! AND THE ICE CHISEL'S BACK AT CAMP!

WHAT WILL I TIE THE.... LINE.....TO?

OKAY SO IT'S NOT BORING, ITS INHUMANE!

MEET OUR PRESIDENT RONALD RAVEN

FOR 80 YEARS HE WAS A PARROT IN PIRATE MOVIES, THEN 50 YEARS AGO HE GOT INTO POLITICS

IT'S ALL SHOW BIZ

AND WOULD YOU BELIEVE HE'S 135 YEARS OLD!

REALLY? HE ONLY LOOKS ABOUT 130 TO ME.

GULP! THIS IS IT!

MY HERO! MY PAL! MY MASTER! I GROVEL AT YOUR FEET!

AND FOR THE MOST HUMILIATING DE-GRADING, DEBASING, FAWNING PERFORMANCE, THE COVETED SYCOPHANT ANTLER AWARD!

RECOGNITION FROM ONE'S PEERS— THE ULTIMATE ACCOLADE!

8

AH, THE LAKE WIND, THE SOUND OF THE WATER!

WE'RE OFF TO FISH CAMP AT LAST! AWAY FROM THE HUSTLE AND BUSTLE OF TOWN! BACK TO THE PEACE AND QUIET OF THE BUSH... YEP, WE'RE LEAVING IT ALL BEHIND....

© D. URQUHART

...(SIGH), WELL SOME OF IT ANYWAY!

NO REALLY I...I HATE SALMON

THEY'RE SLIMEY AND SQUISHY AND VERY BONEY!

INFACT I HOPE I NEVER SEE ANOTHER AS LONG AS I LIVE!

HEY SKOOKUM, WHAT IS THIS?

DUNNO! LOOKS LIKE A CAR BUT THERE'S NO MOTOR AND ITS GOT A GANGLINE IN FRONT

A GANGLINE IN FRONT!!

OH NO! MARTEN'S GONE AND BOUGHT A TRAINING CART!

9

TAIL ERECT, HACKLES UP, AND EARS FORWARD THE THE DOMINANT MALE STARES STRAIGHT AT...

© D. URQUHART

SNARL CRACK CRUNCH SNAP! GRROOWFF! EEEOOW!

TAIL DOWN, EARS BACK AND EYES AVERTED THE SUBORDINATE MALE CRINGES BENEATH...

I'M FROM THE FEDERAL GRANT DEPT. NEED A TRAPPING GRANT? HOUSING GRANT? FUEL GRANT? COFFEE GRANT?

COFFEE GRANT?

IT'S PART OF OUR NEW INTEGRATED SOCIALIZATION AND SMALL BUSINESS PROGRAM WHERE WE PAY YOU A PERCENTAGE OF EACH CUP YOU BUY...

.... JUST FILL OUT THESE FORMS, KEEP THE WHITE ONES, SEND THE PINK ONES TO US, THE BLUE ONES TO THE CAPITAL AND THE GREEN ONES TO YOUR LOCAL GOV'T AGENT...

© D. URQUHART

... LUCKY HE TURNED UP, EH SKOOK? OR I WOULDN'T HAVE THIS TO LIGHT THE DOG POT FIRE WITH!

PACKS ARE HOT, HEAVY AND CUMBERSOME ...(SNARL!) MOST OF THE (SNAP! SNAP!) TIME...

... BUT THEY SURE ..(OOF!) ARE...(OUCH!)... HANDY....

THUD! SWISH SWISH

© D. URQUHART

WHEN YOU HAVE TO THRASH A ⑥✷!!!⑥✷ PORCUPINE!

Panel 1: EVERY YEAR WE COME TO THIS VALLEY WHERE THE CARIBOU MIGRATE PAST WITHOUT FAIL....

Panel 3: SO WHO NEEDS 'EM? WE'LL GO TO A LAKE WHERE EACH YEAR THE MOOSE..

Panel 4: TRAPPING SEASON IS APPROACHING AND EACH YEAR MARTEN..

Panel 5: ..BOILS HIS TRAPS WITH SPRUCE BOUGHS SO THEY'LL SMELL NATURAL AND...

Panel 6: NO FURBEARER CAN DETECT THEM UNDER THE SNOW ...UNLESS....

Panel 7: ...SOME RABID PACIFIST MARKS THEM ALL AFTERWARDS!

HISS HISS

Panel 8: MARTEN IS HELPING THE GAME OFFICER EXPERIMENT WITH HUMANE TRAPS

Panel 9: THEY'RE DESIGNED TO BE QUICK AND MERCIFUL....

SPROING! EEEOOWW!

BUT NOT FOR HUMANS!

14

WE'RE AUDITING YOU TRAPPER SINCE YOU ONLY PAID $300 IN TAXES SINCE 1977!

FIRST YOUR EXPENSES: DOGS, DOG FOOD, SLEDS, TRAPS, SUPPLIES, CABINS, GUNS, BULLETS, NETS, BOAT, OUTBOARD, CHAINSAW, TRUCK, GAS..

NOW, TAKE THAT FROM YOUR EARNINGS AND

.. AHEM... WE OWE YOU $297.63!

1984

THERE'S A LOT TO BEING A BIG GAME GUIDE

TRACKER, CRACK SHOT, COOK, PACKER, SKINNER, WRANGLER — BUT MOST OF ALL A GOOD...

PSYCHIATRIST!

MY WIFE DON' UNNERSTAN' ME! ..MY KIDS DON'... UNNERSTAN' ME!.. (SNIFF!) MY BOSH DON' UNNERSTAN ME! MY...(HIC!)...MISHTRESH DON' UNNERSTAN' ME!.. MY....

WHEN 'SIBERIUS' THE GREAT HUSKY LEADER WAS CROSSING THE ARCTIC...

...THE EXPEDITION RAN OUT OF FOOD AND THE DOGS FINALLY HAD TO **EAT** THEIR MASTER...

ULP!

OF COURSE..(AHEM).. ... TIMES HAVE ... CHANGED...AND...UM THAT COULD **NEVER** HAPPEN NOWADAYS!

THE JIGGER IS A GREAT INVENTION FOR SETTING NETS UNDER THE ICE

THE EXPERT JIGGER DOG FOLLOWS ITS TAPS TO PINPOINT WHERE IT STOPS

TAP! TAP! TAP! TAP!

© D.URQUHART

OF COURSE EVEN EXPERTS HAVE THEIR OFF DAYS!

YOU KNOW MARTEN, BUSH LIFE HAS REALLY OPENED MY EYES!

© D.URQUHART

I FIGURE THAT AS YOUR TRAPPER'S ASSISTANT AND A FISHING GUIDE, I CAN SAVE ENOUGH TO...

... FORM MY OWN ROCK BAND!

84-7

ERNIE'S BACK FROM HIS FIRST TRAPPING TRIP AND THE PUNKS MIGHT RAZZ HIM...

HEY! BUSHMAN! YOU FORGOT TO TAKE YER SNOWSHOES OFF! YUK! YUK! YUK!

HERE'S A PRIME CROSS FOX PELT GLORIA! MAKES NUMBER ONE TRIM!!

OH! ERNEST! IT'S GORGEOUS!

84-8

I GUESS THE KID CAN HANDLE HIMSELF OKAY!

© D.URQUHART

A SNOWMACHINE IS AN EFFICIENT TOOL FOR THE MODERN TRAPPER...

EVEN WHEN IT BREAKS DOWN, A GOOD TRAPPER CAN FIX IT...

...UNLESS HE LACKS THE NECESSARY SPARE PART—IN WHICH CASE IT PAYS...

TO HAVE A FRIEND WITH DOGS!

BOY THIS IS SOME WHITE-OUT! GOOD THING YOUR NOSE CAN LEAD US HOME EH SKOOK?

...SKOOKUM?

SKOOKUM! HELP! OVER HERE BOY!!! SKOOKUM OH GAWD! WHERE ARE YOU!?

RIGHT BESIDE YOU BOSS

THAT'S NOT FUNNY! YOU'VE GOT A VERY SICK PERSONALITY YOU KNOW THAT?

YUP

MARTEN IS CRAZY ABOUT THE IDITAROD! EVERYTHING'S IDITAROD THIS IDITAROD THAT!

INFACT HE'S GONE AND SPENT $4,500 ON THE IDITAROD...

FOR A DISH ANTENNA SO HE CAN WATCH THE RACE ON THE TRAPLINE!

© D. URQUHART

THERE'S ALOT OF PHYSICAL LABOUR IN FRONTIER LIFE

YARD WORK, BUCKING UP FIREWOOD, HAULING WATER, FIXING MOTORS, MENDING BOATS, HANGING NETS, DRYING FISH

YEP, IT'S TOUGH ALRIGHT, BUT SATISFYING...

SO SATISFYING THAT I COULD WATCH IT ALL DAY!

THE HIPPIES ARE WORKING IN TOWN THIS SUMMER AND I HAVEN'T SEEN 'FRISCO IN TWO MONTHS! WONDER IF SHE'S...

A MUM!

YES! AND WHAT'S MORE BIG BOY, YOU'RE THE DAD!

ULP!...BEING A DAD IS A BIG RESPONSIBILITY! I'LL HAVE TO TEACH MY KIDS GOOD FROM EVIL, TRUTH FROM FALSEHOOD AND RIGHT FROM WRONG!

...AND I WILL! ...SOON AS I FIGURE IT OUT FOR MYSELF!

WE COME FLOM JAPAN TO CRIMB MUSH MOUNTAIN!

WHY? IT'S EASY UP THE SOUTH SLOPE

© D. URQUHART

BUT NOBODY EVA CRIMB NOTH FRACE! WE FIRST! GET IN NATRONAL GEO-GLAPHIC, EXPRORERS CRUB, DOCLUMENTRY FRIM!! TOKYO TV TALK SHOW!!! MAYBE GO HORRYWOOD!!

MAYBE I SHOULD'VE TOLD THEM THAT THE NORTH FACE IS UNCLIMBED BECAUSE ITS THE HOME OF OL' SAM THE **KILLER GRIZZLY!**

84-27

OL' SAM'S GOT THE JAPANESE CLIMBERS ON A ROCK IN A **HARD PLACE!**

© D. URQUHART

BUT THE GAME WARDEN CAN'T HELP BECAUSE THE AREA'S SURROUNDED BY **GREEN PEACERS!**

THE ONLY CHANCE IS TO AIR DROP A FEARLESS BEAR DOG TO SCARE OL' SAM OFF

BUT THERE AREN'T ANY IN DOGGEREL...SO ..(ULP!) THEY **CHOSE ME!**

84-28

WELL I'M PAST THE GREEN PEACERS AND THERE'S OL' SAM THE KILLER GRIZZLY

© D. URQUHART

84-29

HI.. S-S-SAM, YOU ...(ULP!) B-BETTER CALL THIS OFF!

WHAT FOR WHITE EYES?

UM...THEY'RE ..UM...FLYING IN..UM...(YES!) YOUR EX-WIFE **OL' GLORIA!** TO REASON WITH YOU!

GLORIA!! C-COMING HERE?!

VAAROOM!

OKAY! EVERYONE IN THIS BAR IS CONSCRIPTED FOR FIREFIGHTING! REPORT TO THE FLOAT DOCK IN ONE HOUR!

CORPORAL PRESTONE'S GETTING SMARTER!

DOGGEREL INN

HE KNEW ABOUT THE FIRE ALL AFTERNOON

BUT WAITED 'TIL **HAPPY HOUR** BEFORE GOING TO THE TAVERN!!

THEY SAY THAT THE LONG COLD NORTHERN WINTERS ARE HARDEST ON PEOPLE...

BUT FOR GUYS LIKE MARTEN AND VICTOR...

SUMMER IS THE SEASON OF **GREATEST STRESS!**

WHAT'S IT LIKE TO FLY?

SAME AS WALKING ONLY HIGHER UP!

BUT DON'T YOU LOVE TO SOAR AND GLIDE?

EAGLES SOAR AND GLIDE! FOR GROUSE IT'S A **FLAPPING NUISANCE!**

WHY NOT WALK THEN?

BECAUSE STUPID! THE ONLY THING SHORTER THAN MY FAT LITTLE WINGS ARE MY SKINNY LITTLE LEGS!!!

OH QUIT YOUR GRIPING!

I'M NOT GRIPING!

I'M ONLY GROUSING!

28

SOUTHERNERS NEED THEIR BIG BANK ACCOUNTS TO FEEL SECURE!

BUT OUR BANK IS THE BUSH WHERE OUR SECURITY IS IN FISH STOCKS, WOOD BONDS, DUCK DEBENTURES AND BIG GAME SAVINGS SUCH AS...

OUR MOOSE ACCOUNT!

...UNT **AXEL** BRINGS MY SLIPPERS, MY PIPE UNT EVEN MY NEWSPAPER!!!

SKOOKUM BEGAN TO LEARN THOSE TRICKS TOO, BUT THEN HE STOPPED

GUESS HE'S NOT AS SMART AS I THOUGHT

THAT'S RIGHT BABY! I'M SMARTER!

MARTEN'S FINALLY GOT HIS ASSISTANT ORGANIZED AND WE'RE READY TO GO

OKAY YOU TAKE THE SLED AND I'LL TAKE THE TOBOGGAN

WELL? WHAT'S THE MATTER NOW?

(ULP!)...WHERE'S THE STARTER SWITCH!

35

SO YOU GUYS FINALLY GAVE UP ON THAT POLYPROPYLENE WIGWAM AND BUILT YOURSELVES A REAL CABIN!

NOT QUITE, WE STILL LIVE IN THE TEEPEE BUT WE SPENT ALL FALL MAKING...

A SAUNA!

VIC'S BEEN MARRIED FOR 10 MONTHS TO PHOEBE BUT SHE'S BEEN AWAY ALL WEEK VISITING HER MOM!

WELL VIC, HOW'S THE BACHELOR LIFE? STAYIN' ALL NIGHT AT THE BAR, FIXIN' YOUR CHAINSAW ON THE KITCHEN TABLE, WATCHIN' ONE GAME ON THE TV AND LISTENING TO ANOTHER ON THE RADIO??!!

ACTUALLY IT'S QUITE LONESOME!!

NORTHERNERS WHO USE FIRES ALL THE TIME DON'T BOTHER WITH BARK AND KINDLING...

ALL YOU NEED IS SOME CHAINSAW GAS, AND A MATCH..... BUT YOU GOTTA BE REAL CAREFUL....

WHUMP!

SEE?.... NOTHIN' TO IT!

36

STOP THE HUNT THERE'S A **CARIBOU CRISIS**!!

BUT LAST YEAR YOU SAID THERE WAS LOTS!

WE MADE A **STATISTICAL ERROR**!!

WELL MAYBE YOU JUST MADE ANOTHER!

POSSIBLY! BUT IT WILL TAKE A YEAR TO FIND OUT!

85-12

THE ENDLESS SAGA OF MEAT-EATERS VS. NUMBER CRUNCHERS!

85-13

VISITING THE OUTHOUSE AT **40 BELOW**!

FT. DOGGEREL IS A PRETTY SIMPLE UNCOMPLICATED KIND OF TOWN!

YUP... ONE BAR, ONE CAFÉ, ONE GROCERY STORE, ONE GAS STATION...

..ONE RIVER, ONE LAKE, ONE SKY, ONE GOD.. AND ONLY...

85-14

...27 DIFFERENT PLACES OF WORSHIP!!!

NORTHERNERS MUST BE SENSITIVE TO THEIR ENVIRONMENT AND FLEXIBLE ENOUGH TO ADJUST THEIR ACTIVITIES TO THE WEATHER....

FOR INSTANCE MARTEN USUALLY WORKS ON THE TRUCK AT 35 BELOW!

.. AND SPLITS WOOD AT 45 BELOW!... BUT WHEN A WARM SPELL COMES ALONG..

..HE'S ALWAYS INSIDE WATCHING THE PLAYOFFS ON TV!!

PHOEBE! GET OVER HERE QUICK!

UNDER... ..THE "B".. FORTY-NINE

ROSIE! ROSIE! YOU CAN'T GO AGAIN TONIGHT!

JUST ONE CARD! I FEEL REALLY LUCKY!

YOU ALWAYS FEEL LUCKY! I KNOW WHAT ITS LIKE .. I'VE BEEN THERE TOO!!

A CRISIS SESSION AT BINGOS ANONYMOUS!

WE REJECT YOUR OFFER OF 2 FISH A DAY AND FRESH STRAW IN OUR HOUSES ONCE A YEAR

LISTEN BUSTER! THIS AIN'T NO FLABBY BUREAUCRACY TO BULLY, OR SOME FAT CITY CORPORATION TO RANSOM!!! ITS JUST A SMALL NORTHERN BUSINESS THAT'S KEEPIN' YOU ALIVE!!!

I THINK '85 WILL BE THE YEAR THAT MANAGEMENT GETS NASTY!

85-21

DON'T WORRY, YOU'RE JUST THE FIRST NEW FACES THEY'VE SEEN IN 8 MONTHS!

I WAS SCARED WHEN I FOUGHT AXEL THE WONDER DOG...

...BUT THAT WAS NOTHING TO THE PANIC OF FACING OL' SAM THE KILLER GRIZZLY..

..AND OL' SAM WASN'T A PATCH ON THE SHEER TERROR OF

CITY TRAFFIC!!

85-22

ONE THING I HATE ABOUT THE CITY...

IS WAITING TO USE A PUBLIC CONVENIENCE!

85-23

YEAH!

GEE GEE! YOU ✦⊙✳ POTLICKER!

WHOA! WHOA! GET GOIN' YOU ✦⊙✳ FLEABAG

A SLED DOG'S LIFE IS NEVER EASY BUT ONE OF MY WORST JOBS IS...

BABYSITTING MARTEN'S NEPHEW!!!

HOW COME THE ROADS ARE STILL DARK?

PLEASE DETAIL YOUR PRIORIZED INITIATIVES AND TIME FRAME FOR THE PROPOSED ILLUMINATION OF FT. DOGGEREL THOROUGHFARES

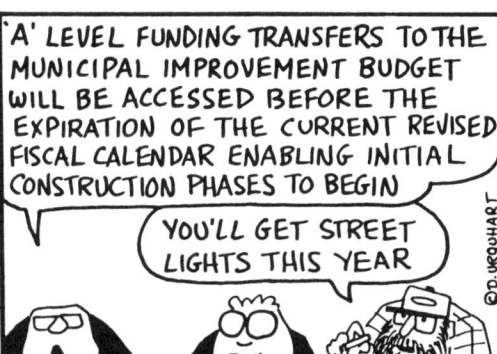

'A' LEVEL FUNDING TRANSFERS TO THE MUNICIPAL IMPROVEMENT BUDGET WILL BE ACCESSED BEFORE THE EXPIRATION OF THE CURRENT REVISED FISCAL CALENDAR ENABLING INITIAL CONSTRUCTION PHASES TO BEGIN

YOU'LL GET STREET LIGHTS THIS YEAR

THINGS SURE GO SMOOTHER WHEN WE BOTH BRING OUR INTERPRETERS!

I LIVED AT DEADLY RAPIDS BEFORE THEY PUT THE ROAD IN...

UM-HMMM, I WAS AT DEADLY RAPIDS BEFORE THEY PUT THE TELEGRAPH IN!

OH YEAH!! WELL I LIVED AT DEADLY RAPIDS BEFORE THEY PUT THE ✦⊙✳!! RAPIDS IN!!

I HATE IT WHEN OLD-TIMERS GET STUCK IN 'RETROBRAGGING MODE'!

43

A SURVIVALIST HAS MOVED TO DOGGEREL AND SPENT A FORTUNE...

...AMASSING 5 YEARS WORTH OF FOOD, WATER, AND AMMO...

..BUT NOW HE'S WORRIED SICK THAT THE NUCLEAR NATIONS WILL...

..FIND A PEACEFUL SOLUTION!

ITS CORPORAL PRESTONE'S THIRD YEAR IN FORT DOGGEREL AND I'LL SAY THIS FOR HIM, HE'S SURE LEARNED ALOT!

HE'S LEARNED NOT TO GO INTO THE BUSH ALONE, NOT TO GO ON THE LAKE ALONE, NOT TO GO INTO THE BAR ALONE, AND NOT TO CLIMB MOUNTAINS ALONE...

INFACT HE'S LEARNED SO MUCH...

THEY'VE MADE HIM A SURVIVAL INSTRUCTOR AT THE ACADEMY!!!

LAST YEAR WE FLEW OUT TO WOLF LAKE AND CANOED THE RAVEN RIVER. GUESS YOU'VE BEEN THERE?

NOPE

AND THE YEAR BEFORE WE HIKED THE RAGGED RANGE TO AXEL GLACIER! GUESS YOU'VE SEEN THAT?

NOPE

HOW LONG HAVE YOU LIVED HERE ANYWAY?

ALL MY ☆⑥✳ LIFE!!

NOTHING BURNS A NORTHERNER MORE THAN BEING TOLD ABOUT HIS OWN COUNTRY BY SOME KNOW-IT-ALL, DONE-IT-ALL TOURISTS!

AH SALMON FISHING! THE HARMONY OF PRIMAL FORCES BINDING MANKIND AND NATURE TOGETHER IN THE PRISTINE NORTHERN ENVIRONMENT!

THE SOCKEYE SEASON IS FROM 10 AM MONDAY TIL 10 AM TUESDAY. YOU CAN'T TAKE KINGS COHOES OR CHINOOKS. MESH SIZE MUST BE 4½ TO 5½ INCHES, NETS 100 YARDS LONG, ONE DRIFTING AND ONE SET OR TWO SET BUT NOT TWO DRIFTING. REPORT YOUR CATCH EVERY 2 HOURS IN TRIPLICATE!

AH SALMON FISHING! THE GOVERNMENT FORCES BINDING FISHERMEN WITH REGULATIONS TO A MODERN BUREAUCRATIC SOCIETY!!

UH-OH!

ARE YOU ALONE?

NO, I HAVE TWO LITTLE CUBS WITH ME!

OKAY WE'LL LEAVE THEN BUT IF YOU WERE BY YOURSELF, I MIGHT HAVE SHOT YOU!!

I KNOW!

THAT'S WHY I LIED!!

AND THIS WAS A QUAINT LITTLE TEA ROOM 'TIL SLY MADE IT INTO A VIDEO PARLOUR, AND THAT WAS AN OLD FOLKS HOME BEFORE SLY BULLDOZED IT FOR AN EQUIPMENT YARD...

BUCKMASTER TOURS

...THAT'S SLY'S EXPLORATION COMPANY WHICH IS REALLY JUST A TAX SHELTER, AND OVER THERE SLY'S BUILDING A DISCO AND BODY RUB...

FISHER YOU'RE FIRED!

LESSON ONE, NEVER HIRE A GUIDE WHO REALLY KNOWS THE PLACE!

47

NOW THERE'S SOUTHERN SOPHISTICATION, A CLASSY DEERSTALKER AND A BRIAR PIPE!

© D. URQUHART

HEY VIC, LOAN ME YOUR CAP AND THAT SOCKET WRENCH

..AND THERE'S ANOTHER TYPICAL NORTHERN NITWIT!!

54-58

I WANTED PARTITIONS SO HE PUT UP STUDS AND GOT NO FURTHER! I WANTED PLUMBING SO HE PUT IN A COLD WATER TAP AND NOTHING MORE! AND FOR ELECTRICITY HE GOT AS FAR AS A TEMPORARY SERVICE AND THAT'S ALL!

INFACT THE ONLY THING HE'S PERSISTENT AT IS...

© D. URQUHART

85-46

MAKING A FAMILY!!!

WITH ONLY GRADE 6 MR. FISHER, YOU'RE NOT QUALIFIED FOR MUCH. WHAT WORK HAVE YOU DONE??

© D. URQUHART

TRAPPER, GUIDE, CARPENTER, LOGGER, FISHERMAN, MECHANIC, MINER, TRUCKER, WELDER, PROSPECTOR, FIRE FIGHTER, CAT SKINNER, LINE CUTTER, STAKER AND BOAT BUILDER.

HOW MANY JOBS HAVE YOU HAD?

ME? JUST THIS ONE BUT IT TOOK 18 YEARS OF EDUCATION TO GET IT!

GEE! MAYBE I GOT OUT OF SCHOOL JUST IN TIME!!

EMPLOYMENT OFFICE

54-47

49

SNOW!? ALREADY! BUT I HAVEN'T PULLED MY NETS, CUT MY FIREWOOD, PAINTED THE SHED, FIXED THE SLED !!!....

48-85

I'M NOT READY FOR WINTER! DO YOU HEAR ME?

OKAY MARTEN YOU'LL GET TWO MORE WEEKS

© D. URQUHART

JEEPERS! I NEVER KNEW THERE REALLY WAS SOMEONE LISTENING UP THERE!

WELL I DID! ... BUT I DIDN'T KNOW HE BOTHERED WITH HUMANS !!

NOW, YOU KNOW THIS HAMBURGER IS SAFE TO EAT BECAUSE IT'S GOT A GOOD GROWTH OF GREY FUNGUS AND GREEN SLIME ON IT.

DUMP

BUT GET THIS! HUMANS WILL EAT THIS RIGHT AFTER IT'S BEEN COOKED! EVEN WHILE IT'S STILL WARM !!!

OH GROSS!! GAG COUGH! RETCH! RALPH !!!

IT'S A SHOCK ALRIGHT! BUT AFTER THEY HEAR ABOUT HUMANS NOTHING ELSE BOTHERS THEM !!

49-85

WELL YOU SLY OLD DOG !!

WHAT?

© D. URQUHART

50-85

ROSIE'S GOING TO HAVE A LITTER!

WHAT!

IS THIS ONE OF YOUR DUMB JOKES!!

NO-O! HONEST!

WHAT'S THE BIG DEAL? HE ONLY HAS TO KEEP WHAT HE WANTS AND SELL THE REST?

...MY GOODNESS MARTEN I NEVER THOUGHT A BACHELOR WOULD HAVE SUCH CLEAN DISHES!! THESE GLASSES SPARKLE!!

DON'T TELL ME **YOU** HAVE A DISHWASHER!

7-86

ACTUALLY I HAVE *FOUR!*

GEE MARTEN— A WHOLE CHINESE MEAL! VERY IMPRESSIVE!!

THANKS! AS A KID I WORKED FOR AN OLD CHINESE GUY WHOSE WIFE HAD A TRAPLINE HERE!

NOW THIS HERE'S LYNX FRIED RICE, SWEET AND SOUR SQUIRREL AND MOOSE EYEBALL SOUP!!

8-86

WATCH NOW! HERE THEY **GO!!!**

9-86

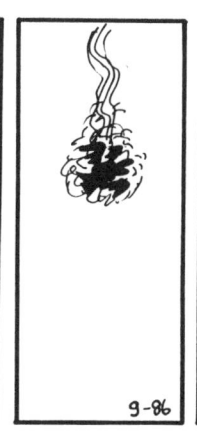

SO THAT'S WHY JAKE THE PILOT WEARS A RAVEN PIN!!!

55

THAT'S THE ANTI-GUN CROWD, THERE'S THE ANTI-HUNTING GROUP, AND THAT'S THE ANTI-TRAPPING LOBBY!

AND WHAT ARE YOU PROTESTING?

NO KILL COMMIES NOT MOOSE

NO I HATE HUNTERS

NO MORE GUNS

TRAPPING MUST STOP!!

10-86

WE'RE HERE TO SAVE AN ENDANGERED SPECIES!!

WHICH ONE?

THE NORTHERNER!

VIC CAN'T MAKE IT!! HE'S WEATHERED IN ON THE TRAPLINE!!

11-86

WELL, GET SOME OTHER CLOSE FRIEND TO DO IT!

BUT...I ONLY HAVE ONE OTHER...

OKAY! OKAY! GET HIM THEN!!

©D. URQUHART

THE RING PLEASE

ROSIE! ROSIE! THROW YOUR BOUQUET!!!

12-86

NOOO... NOOOOO..

C'MON HONEY, WE'LL NEVER GET OUTA HERE!

©D. URQUHART

56

SKOOKUM'S BELIEVE IT OR ELSE!

13-86   ©D.URQUHART

THE MOST IMPORTANT BUSH SURVIVAL TOOL IS NOT MATCHES OR A COMPASS OR A RIFLE.... BUT......

TOILET PAPER!

..AMONG ITS MANY NORTHERN USES ARE:

BUSH NAPKIN   TRAP SETTER   GUN CLEANER   WIND STREAMER

BUSH HANKY   FIRE STARTER   PLUG DRIER   AND...OF COURSE

WOOPS! LOOKS LIKE ANOTHER ROADSIDE TOKEN

WHAT'S THAT?

A HUSKY THAT SOME SOUTHERN TRENDY GOT AS THEIR TOKEN SLED DOG. BUT WHEN THEY HEAD SOUTH AGAIN, THE ARCTIC BEAST DOESN'T FIT THEIR LIFESTYLE!

14-86

THAT'S HOW MY BROTHER GOT INTO THIS BUSINESS!!

RENT A HUSKY

A MUST FOR THE URBAN ARCTIC TRENDY...GOOD AS A JOGGING COMPANION, BACKYARD DISPLAY, TRUCK PASSENGER

COLLARS AND SLEDS EXTRA

THIS TEST WILL HURT A BIT, MARTEN, BUT ITS NECESSARY... ARE YOU READY??

YEAH

15-86

FIRE DEPARTMENT, TOWN COUNCIL, REC CENTRE, GUN CLUB...

HUH? NO!! NO! NO!

BOARD OF TRADE, HISTORICAL SOCIETY, SCHOOL BOARD...

AGGHH! NO! STOP! STOP!

A CLASSIC CASE OF **VOLUNTEER BURN-OUT!**

57

EVOLUTIONISTS SAY MEN CAME FROM MONKEYS, RAVENS FROM LIZARDS AND HUSKIES HAVE EVOLVED FROM THE **MIGHTY WOLF!**

BUT CREATIONISTS SAY THAT MAN IS THE HEAD HONCHO, AND THE REST OF US ARE JUST HIS **TOYS!!!**

WELL, YOU CAN ALWAYS COUNT ON GRIZZ FOR A CLEAR UNBIASED PRESENTATION OF TRICKY TOPICS!

YOU KNOW? I ALMOST FORGOT WHAT THIS IS LIKE!!!

IN NAMING A CHILD, IT'S OFTEN HELPFUL TO THINK OF NAMES THAT HAVE BEEN IMPORTANT IN YOUR OWN LIFE...

MARTEN? CAN YOU THINK OF ANY??

ME?.. WELL ...UM...... LET'S SEE...

MERCURY, EVINRUDE JOHNSON, GRUMANN, CHESTNUT, HUSQVARNA, STIHL, SILVA, COLEMAN, BROWNING, WINCHESTER, REMINGTON, BUSHNELL, TASCO...

GOIN' OUT TO CHOP KINDLING

HMM... THAT SHOULD BE IN THE SHED

GOSH! I BETTER GO MAIL THIS ORDER!!

MARTEN! CAN YOU HELP ME DELIVER THIS LOADER TO MOOSE BERRY?

YOU WENT OUT TO GET KINDLING AND NOW YOU'RE CALLING FROM ANOTHER TOWN?

28-86

OKAY THAT'S THE LAST ONE.... GOT IT ??

YUP... MOOSE HOOF UNDER THE LOG

IT'S SURE HELL TO BE OLD!!

NOW I HAVE TO PAY A PUP TO REMEMBER WHERE MY BONES ARE BURIED!!

29-86

THIS LOAD IS TOO BIG FOR THE BEAVERS

BETTER SEND THE OTTERS OR MAYBE EVEN THE TWIN OTTERS

HELLO? HELLO? GREEN PEACE?

TELEPHONE

THESE NORTHERNERS ARE ENSLAVING WILDLIFE TO DO FORCED LABOUR!

30-86

HERE COME THE SCIENTISTS!

37-86

© D. URQUHART

WE'RE CONDUCTING A SEASONAL MOOD STUDY... PLEASE RECORD YOUR FEELINGS!

OH WELL, YOU KNOW.. ..IT'S SUMMERTIME

FISH ARE JUMPIN'..

..AND THE LIVIN' IS EASY...

..AND THE COTTON-GRASS IS HIGH....

MY!! SOME OF THESE RUSTICS HAVE A VERY LYRICAL WAY OF EXPRESSING THEMSELVES!

YES! ALMOST LIKE MUSIC!

WE'RE THE BEST OF FRIENDS AREN'T WE PHOEBE?

THE BEST ROSIE!

WE SHARE SECRETS ABOUT OUR LIVES...

OUR DREAMS..

OUR HUSBANDS..

OUR PRIVATE BERRY PATCHES!

OF COURSE!

FOR SURE!

NATURALLY!

38-86

© D. URQUHART

PHOEBE??

ROSIE... NO FRIENDS ARE *THAT* CLOSE!!!

SKOOKUM'S TRUE NORTH LORE

FOR CENTURIES MEN HAVE BEEN RELENTLESSLY HUNTING AND TRAPPING BEAVER, BUT LATELY THE BEAVER HAVE BEEN GETTING BACK THEIR REVENGE....

© D. URQUHART

39-86

BEAVER FEVER!

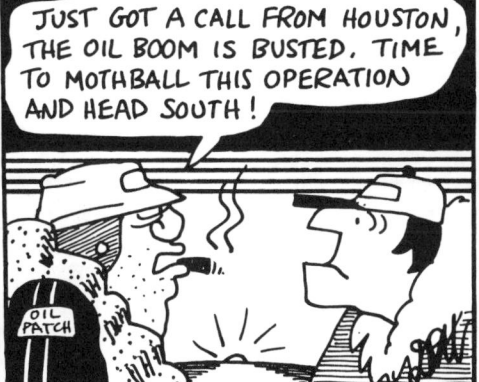

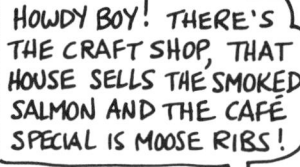

WELL, HERE COMES THE GOVERNMENT FRONT MAN WITH HIS SHINY NEW ATTACHÉ CASE. JEEPERS! THEY'RE DRAFTING KIDS! I BET HE'S NEVER EVEN FIRED OFF A MEMO!!

HOWDY BOY! THERE'S THE CRAFT SHOP, THAT HOUSE SELLS THE SMOKED SALMON AND THE CAFÉ SPECIAL IS MOOSE RIBS!

I'D LIKE TO HIRE A GUIDE AND VISIT A TRAPLINE... ALSO BUY A FEW PUPS TO START MY OWN DOG TEAM...

52-86

SON... HOW DID YOU SLIP THROUGH THE SYSTEM?

© D. URQUHART

WELL GENTLEMEN... YOUNG MANDARIN IS BACK FROM FT. DOGGEREL, WE'D BETTER DEBRIEF HIM BEFORE HE DOES SOMETHING DECISIVE!!

DEPARTMENT OF BUREAUCRACY

MISS STONEWALL? SEND MANDARIN IN PLEASE!

© D.URQUHART

OH MY GAWD!

53-86

THEY GOT TO HIM!!

BOY! ROSIE WILL BE PLEASED WITH THIS BEAUTIFUL YOUNG BULL WE GOT!!

GEE...THERE'S OLD LADY FLINT, BET SHE'D LIKE THE HEART!...AND WHAT ABOUT UNCLE MOSS WHO'S TOO OLD TO HUNT?

...AND THE WIDOW PIKE ...AND THE FOXE FAMILY'S ON WELFARE ...AND THE KIDS AT THE HOSTEL SURE MISS WILD MEAT!

54-86

SUPRISE DEAR! WE GOT US A 'GREAT MOOSE......RACK!!

© D.URQUHART

70

HOW DO YOU STAY SO YOUNG SKIDDER?

LIFE'S ALOT LIKE LOGGING MARTEN! I DON'T PINE AWAY FOR LOST LOVES...

BUT SPRUCE UP AND BRANCH OUT, ALWAYS LOOKING FIR MY ALDER EGO TO TIE THE KNOT!!

BUT THE REAL SECRET IS...

SERIAL MAHOGANY!

GWEN
SALLY
BELLE
RITA

OH NO! NOT THIS CRUD AGAIN! I WON'T EAT IT! I'LL STARVE FIRST!

RAARR!

CHOMP GOBBLE!
GULP GULP!

PRESIDENT RAVEN, HAVE YOU LEARNED ANYTHING FROM IRANGATE!

WELL, OLLIE SEEMED LIKE A RELIABLE YOUNG RAVEN...

BUT I SHOULD HAVE KNOWN HE'D BE NOT ONLY CLEVER AND INTREPID BUT ALSO DEVIOUS, UNGOVERNABLE AND CUNNING...

WITH A NAME LIKE NORTH!

72

MARTEN AND ROSIE ARE HAVING A VERY SOPHISTICATED PARTY!

EVERYONE'S DRESSED IN THE LATEST MAIL ORDER FASHIONS!

...BUT YOU CAN ALWAYS TELL A NORTHERN PARTY...

NO SHOES!

GOOD GRIEF! SOMEONE'S GONE CRAZY WITH THE SURVEY TAPE AGAIN!

HEY! WHY DO YOU KEEP TAPING EVERY ★G※! TREE ON THIS TRAIL!

WE'RE AFRAID WE'LL LOSE OUR WAY!

WELL MARTEN, YOU THINK YOUNG WINCHESTER WILL BE A DOG MUSHER LIKE HIS OLD MAN?

I USED TO...

...UNTIL HE NAMED THE PUPS...

...'SKIDOO', 'YAMAHA', 'POLARIS' AND 'MOTOSKI'!!!

74

MARTEN! THERE'S A FIFTY DOLLAR BILL TACKED TO THE BULLETIN BOARD!!!

YEAH, THEY FOUND IT AFTER THE LAST MOVIE AND NOBODY HAS CLAIMED IT YET!

I BET IT WAS THE HIGHWAYS INSPECTOR OR THAT BIG GUY WHO BOUGHT JAKE'S CLAIMS...

WELL SOME SAY IT WAS UNDER THE DOCTORS SEAT BUT I THINK...

THIS COMMUNITY IS SICK!!

WE'RE A SIMPLE BUSH FAMILY! WE DON'T NEED A DISHWASHER!

OH YEAH? YOU GET FIREWOOD WITH A CHAINSAW AND A FOUR-BY-FOUR!

THAT'S COMPLETELY DIFFERENT!

...ON THE OTHER HAND...

...AND IF YOU ENDORSE OUR PLAN, YOU CAN QUIT THOSE PART TIME BUSH JOBS...

NORTHERN ECONOMIC INITIATIVES

...AND ALL BE WORKING FULL TIME, 9 TO 5, FIVE DAYS A WEEK 50 WEEKS A YEAR!!

WHAT DID I SAY?!

ADRIFT ON A SMALL FLOE IN THE BEAUFORT SEA... VITUS BERING SCANS THE HORIZON FOR LAND...

...HIS HUSKIES CLINGING DESPERATELY TO HIM AS COLD AND HUNGER SINK IN..

WHO EVER SAID BREAK-UP WAS DULL?!

THE OLD DOGGEREL ROAD IS SO PRETTY....

THE DEPARTMENT OF HIGHWAYS IS UPGRADING IT!

OLD DOGGEREL SCENIC ROUTE PROJECT

WELL IT TOOK 250 YEARS BUT AT LAST I'M THE TALLEST TREE IN THE BUSH!

AND DESPITE WHAT THEY SAY...

IT AIN'T LONLEY AT THE TOP!

BLURK!

BUT YOU SURE GET DUMPED ON ALOT!

IN THE DEPARTMENT OF BUREAUCRACY

MANDARIN! WHAT'S THIS BUSH SURVIVAL FOR BUREAUCRATS COURSE YOU BUDGETED FOR??

GREAT SCOTT MAN! WE'RE SUPPOSED TO BE **CIVILIZING** THE NORTHERN RUBES NOT THE OTHER WAY ROUND!!

YOU'VE GONE AND GOT THAT FORT DOGGEREL RENEGADE MARTEN FISHER TO PLANT **PINKOS** IN OUR RANKS!!

© D. URQUHART   27-87

..SO I'M SENDING MY THREE BEST MEN TO KEEP AN EYE ON THINGS!

TO BE CONTINUED....

DAY ONE OF BUSH SURVIVAL (B.S.) FOR BUREAUCRATS....

WELCOME TO THE MARTEN FISHER GREEN GARBAGE BAG SCHOOL OF BUSH SURVIVAL

FIRST WE TAKE AWAY ALL YOUR L.L. BEAN, EDDIE BAUER AND MOUNTAIN COOP JUNK...

...AND GIVE YOU REAL GEAR FROM OUR GENERAL STORE... SNEAKERS, BALL CAPS, KOREAN MACKINAWS, JEANS, TOILET PAPER, TEA AND LOTS OF **GREEN GARBAGE BAGS!**

© D. URQUHART   28-87

HE'S GOING TO **KILL US!!**

TO BE CONTINUED...

THE NOW FAMOUS GREEN GARBAGE BAG LECTURE...   29-87

REMEMBER PAPER PEOPLE, A MAN ALONE IN THE BUSH WITH 20 GREEN GARBAGE BAGS FEARS NOTHING!

SO STUDY THIS DEMONSTRATION OF USES LIKE: FISH NET FLOATS, BUCKET, DUFFEL BAG, PACK SACK LINER, GUN CASE, MEAT PROTECTOR, BIVOUAC COVER RAIN HAT AND VEST, FISH GUTTING-APRON, FLAGGING AND WINDSOCK..

© D. URQUHART

TO BE CONTINUED...

82

83

WHATCHA DOING?

STORING MUSHROOMS FOR WINTER

BUT YOU EAT ONLY DOG FOOD FROM OUR YARD?

YEAH! BUT THIS IS MY **CULTURAL HERITAGE** I CAN'T LOSE TOUCH WITH MY **ROOTS!!**

ULP! MAYBE HE'S GOT A POINT!

TO BE CONTINUED...

ALL HUSKIES ARE BROTHER TO THE WOLF...

SKOOKUM PONDERS HIS ROOTS...

DEEP IN OUR WILD HEARTS NOTHING IS BETTER THAN A FRESH MOOSE HAUNCH DRIPPING WITH BLOOD!

UNLESS IT'S A DOUBLE CHOCOLATE DIPPED ROCKY ROAD IN A SUGAR CONE

IT'S HOPELESS! I'VE NO ROOTS! I EAT JUNK FOOD, TAKE TRUCK RIDES AND LIVE IN A PLYWOOD HOUSE!

HEY MY MAN! I'LL TELL YOU ABOUT **ROOTS!**

IT'S YOUR LOVE OF THE NORTH! THE SNOW THE WILDLIFE! THE SCENERY! ADVENTURE AND FREEDOM! THAT'S WHAT YOU SHARE WITH YOUR ANCESTORS!

YEAH!.... AND ONE THING ELSE!

WHAT'S THAT?

A CRAZY BELIEF IN **TALKING TREES!**

BOY! THIS LAKE IS SO REMOTE THE MOOSE HAVE NEVER EVEN SEEN A HUMAN BEFORE!!

??

FLEE! FLEE! A KILL CRAZED PSYCOPATH WITH A GUN!

45-87

© D.URQUHART

BUT THE ✻@ DUCKS HAVE!

OKAY, I'LL THRASH THE WILLOWS, GIVE A FEW GRUNTS AND RUSH YOU!

RIGHT! THEN WE LOCK ANTLERS SNORT, PUSH...THEN I'LL TAKE A FALL AND LEAVE!

46-87

PRO WRESTLING IS A SHAM BUT THE LADIES LOVE IT!

ED AND BETH ARE LEAVING. THINK I SHOULD BUY HIS D-4?

NOPE! IT'S PROBABLY A BOOMERANG MOVE!

47-87

OKAY, WHAT'S A BOOMERANG MOVE?

YOU KNOW, PEOPLE DECIDE THEY HATE DOGGEREL, AND MOVE DOWN SOUTH BUT THEN A COUPLE OF YEARS LATER

©D.URQUHART

THEY'RE ON YOUR DOORSTEP PLEADING TO BUY THEIR STUFF BACK AGAIN!!

85

THE ANCIENT GREEKS CALLED THOSE STARS URSA MAJOR AND URSA MINOR — THE BIG BEAR AND LITTLE BEAR...

59-87

BUT NORTHERNERS CALL THEM THE BIG DIPPER AND LITTLE DIPPER...

WHY?

PROBABLY BECAUSE THE ANCIENT GREEKS WERE HEAVY THINKERS...

BUT THE OLD TIME NORTHERNERS WERE HEAVY DRINKERS!

IT'S A LOT DIFFERENT THAN I EXPECTED!

MARTEN... MARRIAGE IS LIKE A DOG TEAM...

THERE'S THE DREAM...

IDITAROD

60-87

..AND THE REALITY!

© D. URQUHART

...YEAH...BUT I STILL CAN'T TIE MY WIFE BEHIND THE SLED WHEN SHE'S ACTING UP!

61-87

DO YOU LIKE GOING OUT ON SLED TRIPS?

SURE, YES, OF COURSE!

© D. URQUHART

DO YOU LIKE BEING CHAINED UP AT HOME?

NO! NEVER! NOT AT ALL!

THEN WHY DO YOU PULL HARDER ON THE WAY HOME THAN ON THE WAY OUT?

?!

BOY! HE'S BEEN ASKING SOME TOUGHIES LATELY! SUPPOSE HE'S WRITING A BOOK?

89

1988

NOVEMBER

BOY! YOU CAN'T DEPEND ON THE WEATHER NOWADAYS!! THAT THERE **EL NINO** SURE SCREWED THINGS UP!!!

NO SNOW, POOR FUR, OPEN LAKES!!! IN THE OLD DAYS YOU COULD COUNT ON A GOOD FIVE MONTHS OF 20 - 40 BELOW!!!

JANUARY

9-88

REAL BRASS MONKEY DAY, EH MARTEN? WHAT HAPPENED TO EL NINO? CAN'T DEPEND ON NOTHIN' NOWADAYS!!!

UH-OH! A SNOWDRIFT IN DISTRESS!!

OOO!.. ACHH! OWCH!!!

10-88

HANG ON THERE! RELIEF IS AT HAND!

A LITTLE TO THE LEFT ..! AHHH! THERE! THANKS!

SNOW FLEAS!

MARTEN! YOU'RE SPENDING A FORTUNE ON THOSE SCRATCH AND WINS!!

HEY! I'M A LUCKY GUY!! MY LUCK WILL CHANGE SOON!!!

SCRATCH! SCRATCH!..

LOOK! SOMEONE DROPPED AN UNUSED TICKET IN THE SNOW!!

© D. URQUHART

I WON! I WON $1500!!

SCRATCH! SCRATCH!!

LAS VEGAS RULE #1: NEVER BACK A LOSER BECAUSE HIS LUCK IS BOUND TO CHANGE!

11-8

93

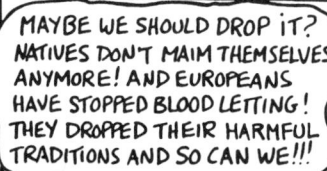

SOMETIMES WOLF CONTROL IS NECESSARY, BUT MARTEN DISAGREES WITH THIS PROJECT, SO HE AND VIC HIRED ON AS GOVERNMENT HUNTERS

TERMINATOR ONE THIS IS LUPUS BASE HOW'S THE WOLF HUNTING?

ROGER BASE! WE ALREADY GOT A PACK OF 6...

AND KILLED THEM ALL!!

ACH! THOSE SILLY NATIVE DOGS! THEY SAY HUSKY BREEDS ARE NAMED AFTER ABORIGINAL TRIBES IN RUSSIA!!

WHEN I **KNOW** THEY WERE BRED BY FAMOUS KLONDIKERS **SAM OYED**, **AL AMUTE** AND **CY BERIAN**!!

© D. URQUHART 28-88

SO! HOW'S ABOUT THAT THERE **HOLOCAUST**? WHAT A **HOAX**, EH?

OH MARY! I'M SO SO SORRY!

YEAH OL' BUDDY! WHAT CAN I SAY?!

WHAT'S WRONG? BANKRUPTCY DIVORCE? TERMINAL ILLNESS? SUDDEN DEATH?

THEY MIGHT AS WELL BE DEAD!

THEY HAVE TO MOVE DOWN SOUTH!

OH GRIZZLED ONE! TELL US ABOUT LIFE AND DEATH!

IN THE HUSKY WORLD LIFE AND DEATH COME FULL CIRCLE, WE EAT FISH...

...FISH EAT MOSQUITOES AND...

MOSQUITOES EAT US!!

OH WHAT A BEAUTIFUL SPOT! TOO BAD SOMEONE WRECKED IT BY BUILDING ON IT!!

OH WHAT A BEAUTIFUL SPOT!

LET'S BUILD A CABIN HERE!!!

AND AUNTIE AND HER 4 KIDS ARRIVE TONIGHT FOR A TWO WEEK VISIT, AND MY SISTER IS DUE IN TOMORROW..

SKOOK? REMEMBER ASKING WHY I MADE YOU AN EXTRA BIG DOGHOUSE?

WELL, NOW YOU KNOW!

CAMP COOKING STINKS! A DOZEN SEX-STARVED MINERS GOGGLING AT YOU EVERY DAY AND MAKING PASSES AT YOU EVERY NIGHT!

DOESN'T IT DISGUST YOU?!

42-88

OH MY YEESS!!

?

WAIT NOW! WAIT NOW! OKAY? READY!?

OKAY!! GO!! GO!! GO! GO! GO!!

SPLAT!!!

43-88

OH WELL!! TOO BAD!!

IS THIS OUR JAR?

NO! PHOEBE GAVE IT TO ME FULL OF ROSEHIP SYRUP SO I FILLED IT WITH MOOSE PATE FOR HER..

44-88

AND SHE RETURNED IT WITH CROWBERRY JAM SO I'M SENDING IT BACK WITH MARINATED SALMON...

A NORTHERN GLITCH IN THE MODERN THROW-AWAY SOCIETY!

105

LISTEN SCUM! I SHOULD BOOT YOUR SKINNY BUTT INTO NEXT WEEK!

AND THEN TEAR OUT YOUR THROAT AND FEED YOUR LIVER TO THE SLED DOGS!!

BUT I AIN'T GONNA!

WH-WH WHY?

'CAUSE GRANDMA SAID SO!

ELDERS, THE U.N. OF THE NORTH!

48-88

SKOOKUM'S NORTHERN Lexicon:

Coors LIGHT
"NORTHERN LIGHTS"

"SUN DOGS"

Solidämosh
"MAGNETIC POLE"

"PHLEBITIS"

"MICROWAVE"

"RV DUMP"

49-88

GOT THE BEER?... WHISKEY? NACHOS?... TAPES...

...YEP! ...YEP! ...YEP! ...YEP!

CARDS?... DUSTERS?... SMOKES?...

...YEP! ...YEP! ...YEP!

50-88

WHAT ON EARTH ARE YOU GUYS DOING??!!

GOIN' HUNTING OF COURSE!

109

ULP! THIS IS A FIRST IN CARTOON HISTORY!!

© D.URQUHART 07-89

OUR CARTOONIST HAS JUST DRAWN HIMSELF INTO OUR STRIP!

WHAT ARE YOU DOING HERE?

I'VE GOT SOME BAD NEWS SKOOK! AND I WANTED TO TELL YOU IN PERSON

TO BE CONTINUED...

I HAVE TO SUSPEND THE STRIP!!

CANCEL US? WHY?

08-89

I HAVE TO GET AWAY FOR AWHILE!

AWAY? FROM WHAT?

FROM THE YUPPIES! THEY'RE INVADING THE NORTH! STRANGLING THE FUR INDUSTRY, LOBBYING FOR GUN CONTROL! PROMOTING THE GREAT INDOORS WITH AEROBICS AND COMPUTERS! TURNING THE OUTDOORS INTO AN EQUIPMENT SHOWPLACE!

© D.URQUHART

RECENTLY A CLOSE FRIEND BECAME A YUPPY RIGHT BEFORE MY EYES!!

09-89

ONE WEEK HE WAS TRAINING HIS TEAM FOR THE YUKON QUEST...

AND THE NEXT WEEK HE SOLD THEM ALL FOR A MACKINTOSH WITH A MOUSE AND A LAZER PRINTER...

JUST TO WRITE LETTERS!

110

1990

114

115

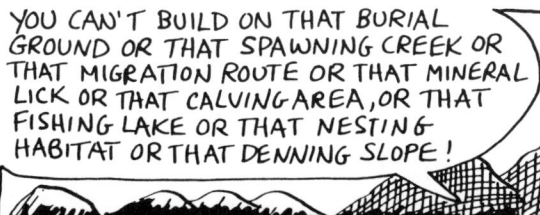

TO GET THE PLANE OFF THIS LITTLE LAKE, THEY TIED IT TO A TREE AND AFTER ITS REALLY REVVED UP... I CHEW THROUGH THE ROPE...

RARR! RARR!

...A CLASSIC NORTHERN SOLUTION... ONLY ONE PROBLEM THOUGH...

RRRAAAARR!

SNAP!

I'M 60 G✳︎ MILES FROM HOME!

90-22

OKAY ROSIE! WHAT DO YOU RUB INTO A MOOSE HIDE TO SOFTEN IT?

OH THAT'S EASY! BRAINS!

MARTEN NAME 6 TRAPPING LURES

BEAVER CASTOR, FISH OIL, MINK MUSK, CATNIP, ANISE,...AND ASAFOETIDA!!

PHOEBE WHAT'S THE BEST RIFLE FOR HUNTING SEALS?

.3030? NO! WAIT! .22? NO! A.222 RIGHT?

90-23

TRADITIONAL PURSUITS ®

THANKS FOR MAKING TEA HONEY BUT IT TASTES KIND OF WEIRD!

OH IT'S SOME ORIENTAL STUFF VIC GAVE ME

90-24

SO? HOW DO YOU FEEL?

FINE WHY?

YOU'RE SURE? HOW ABOUT MORE TEA?

I'M FINE? NO MORE TEA! WHAT'S GOT INTO YOU?

NO LUCK HERE EITHER! GUESS WE BETTER TAKE THOSE VELVET CARIBOU ANTLERS TO THE DUMP!

© D. URQUHART

118

119

MARTEN HAS ARRANGED A SECRET MEETING WITH MR. SUN AND THE FORT DOGGEREL SHAMAN...

HELLO? ANYBODY HOME?

90-28

MR. SUN I GIVE YOU POWERFUL LOVE POTION MADE FROM TAIL OF THE MUSKRAT...SEE HOW IT AFFECT THESE WOMANS!!!

OH! MR. SUN!! YOU'RE SOOO SEXY!!

YO! BRO! CANCEL ALLA ANTLER ORDERS WE GONNA CORNER THE FUTURES MARKET IN MUSKRAT TAILS!

THANKS LADIES!!

©D.URQUHART

GO BACK PAST THE CHURCH AND TURN RIGHT AT THE LITTLE GREY HOUSE!

SO? IS THAT FOURTH STREET OR FIFTH AVENUE?

HOW WOULD WE KNOW? WE WERE **BORN HERE!**

©D.URQUHART

GUESS THAT MAKES SENSE **TO NORTHERNERS!**

90-29

SKOOKUM'S **C**IENCE **S**ERIES...

"FOR DECADES BIOLOGISTS WERE PUZZLED BY THE FALL REVERSAL OF CARIBOU MIGRATIONS[1]."

TREE LINE

"THEN RECENTLY TWO BIOLOGISTS FOUND THAT DURING THE FALL CARIBOU GORGE ON MUSHROOMS[2].

"BUT IT TOOK TWO BUSH MASTERS TO SHOW SCIENTISTS THAT THE WEIRD FALL MIGRATIONS ARE SIMPLY BECAUSE."

"...THE CARIBOU ARE **STONED**[3]!!"

ARE WE GOIN' SUNTH? SO2? SOUS?

OOOO! LOOK! THREE SUNS!!

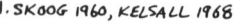

1. SKOOG 1960, KELSALL 1968   2. MARTELL & RUSSELL 1989   90-30   3. FISHER & SKOOKUM 1990

SO I'LL PUT THIS HERE TO PICK UP ON MY WAY TO THE SHOP AND THIS CAN STAY UNTIL I GO DOWN TO THE LAKE...

..AND I'LL PUT THESE TOGETHER TO TAKE OVER TO VIC LATER, AND THIS CAN GO HERE UNTIL I GET THE TRUCK...

MARTEN! WHAT ARE YOU DOING OUT THERE?!!

WHAT'S IT LOOK LIKE? I'M TIDYING UP!!!

90-31

ISN'T IT STRANGE THAT ALDER CONES LOOK JUST LIKE SPRUCE CONES?!

90-32

THAT'S BECAUSE WE EVOLVED 100 MILLION YEARS EARLIER AND YOU COPIED FROM US!

DID NOT!

© D. URQUHART

DID SO! DID SO! DID SO!!

DID NOT! DID NOT! DID NOT!

ALDERCATIONS!

UH-OH! COFFEE BREAK!!!

ROAR! CRASH! CRACK!

© D. URQUHART

AH! AIN'T NATURE BEAUTIFUL!!

90-33

SKOOK! YOU GOTTA HELP ME ESCAPE FROM AN OUTFITTER! HE STARVES US AND LOADS US DOWN WITH FAT HUNTERS!!

©D.URQUHART

UH-OH! THERE'S HIS SUPERCUB! HE'LL SPOT ME FOR SURE!

QUICK! LIE DOWN!

DANG! THE WOLVES ALREADY GOT OLD BLAZE THERE'S ONE STILL CHEWIN' ON HIM!

90-34

WELL WE BETTER GET BACK TO CAMP AND PUT THAT FAT OLD HERMAN GUY ON BESS!

WHAT A GREAT FEELING!!! IMAGINE FINDING A PLACE...

©D.URQUHART

...WITH ABSOLUTELY NO SIGNS OF HUMANS!! HEY WE COULD BE THE FIRST PEOPLE TO SET FOOT HERE!!

90-35

LET'S BUILD A CAIRN!!

MARTEN IS HELPING TO NAME LOCAL LANDMARKS

.."AND THIS IS "MARTEN LAKE" AND THIS IS "MARTEN MOUNTAIN" AND THIS IS "MARTEN CREEK"...

90-36

MARTEN! I'M TELLING HIM THOSE NAMES ARE ALL FALSE!!!

©D.URQUHART

..AND THIS IS "ROSIE LAKE" AND THIS IS "ROSIE RIVER" AND THIS IS "ROSIE RIDGE".

AMAZING HOW THIS OLD GUY SURVIVED HUNDREDS OF YEARS MORE THAN THE REST!

BECAUSE I WAS TOO SHORT FOR TEEPEE POLES, TOO TAPERED FOR CABIN LOGS, TOO TWISTED FOR SPLITTING AND TOO KNOTTY FOR CARVING!

90-37

SO AFTER EVERYONE ELSE GOT USED UP OR BURNT OUT, I BECAME EXECUTIVE DIRECTOR!

YOU MAY BE EMPHASIZING WINCHESTER'S MECHANICAL ABILITY TOO MUCH.

BECAUSE WHEN I ASKED THE CLASS FOR AN AUTOBIOGRAPHY, HE...

90-38

..WROTE A LIFE HISTORY OF **YOUR TRUCK!**

MY DaDz 4x4

an Auto Biography by "WINCH" FISHER

"PAD A CLAIM PAD A CLAIM PROSPECTOR MAN"

90-39

MAKE ME A FORTUNE AS FAST AS YOU CAN"

"STAKE IT AND DRILL IT AND SALT IT WITH GOLD"

"AND SELL IT DOWN SOUTH AS THE MOTHER LODE"

123

GAWD! I'M OFF ON A 300 MILE DRIVE AT -40° WITH A COUPLE OF FORT DOGGEREL LOCALS...

THEY SAID NOT TO WORRY ABOUT SURVIVAL GEAR BUT THEIR TRUCK BOX LOOKS **EMPTY**!

HEY! YOU SAID YOU'D TAKE CARE OF **SURVIVAL** ON THIS TRIP!!!

WE DID! MEET CHARLIE JOHN PETER! NINETY-FIVE WINTERS IN THE BUSH AND HE SURVIVED EVERY ONE!!

I'M DEAD! MARTEN'S TRUCK BROKE DOWN A 120 MILES FROM TOWN AT 45° B·B·BELOW...

...AND NOW WE'RE WADING THROUGH THE SNOW AND DARK BEHIND A 100-YEAR-OLD INDIAN BECAUSE HE SAW 3 RAVENS FLY INTO THE BUSH HERE!!

CABIN AHEAD

YOU'RE A MIRACLE! A GENIUS! A SAVIOUR!

ACTUALLY THIS IS MY WIFE'S BROTHER'S SON'S TRAPLINE!!

I WISH YOU GUYS WOULD CLEAN YOUR OWN YARDS!!!

LISTEN! HUSKIES EVOLVED TO RUN AND PULL! HUMANS EVOLVED TO USE SHOVELS! HEY, IF I COULD USE A SHOVEL, I'D DO IT!!!

ACTUALLY HUMANS ONLY EVOLVED TO OUTSMART **OTHER ANIMALS!**

WHY ARE PACKAGES DIFFERENT SHAPES? 91-6

WELL, FOR BUSH USE OF COURSE!

"BLEACH BOTTLES FOR BOAT BAILERS..."

AND NET FLOATS"

"COKE CANS FOR COOKIE CUTTERS"

"LARD PAILS FOR TEA BILLIES..."

...AND BERRIES"

"KETCHUP BOTTLES FOR SPIN CASTERS"

"GARBAGE BAGS FOR RAIN GEAR"

"AND PAMPERS FOR SNOW GOOSE DECOYS"

GEE, BIG BUSINESS REALLY CATERS TO US NORTHERNERS!

HE'LL LEARN THE TRUTH SOON ENOUGH!

BOY! 60 BELOW AND WE'RE TRAVELLING AT 70 MPH!! 91-7

YEAH! SO THE WIND CHILL OUT THERE MUST BE SOMETHING **AWESOME!**

TELL ME ABOUT IT!

Dear Uncle Marten:
The recruiter asked if I was a good driver...

91-8

I said, "Hell I'm a Northerner!! I can drive 90 mph on icy roads with only a little hole in a frosted window to see through!"

So they put me in the tank corps!!!

©D. URQUHART

129

130

REMEMBER FRANK?

WHO?

THE GUY WHO ALWAYS BRAGGED ABOUT BEING SO TALL AND STRAIGHT?

OH! YEAH! SO WHAT ABOUT HIM?

91-16

WELL I THINK HE'S BACK!!

©D. URQUHART

WE NEED A CHANGE OF SCENE!!!

WE COULD MOVE!!

TO THE COAST?

BACK EAST?

DOWN SOUTH

TOO WET!

TOO FLAT!

TOO CROWDED!!

I'VE GOT IT!!

91-17 LET'S BUY THE OLD FROST PLACE NORTH OF TOWN! I ALWAYS LIKED THAT VIEW!!!

ONCE A NORTHERNER ALWAYS A NORTHERNER!

THERE'S ARNIE! I'LL GET HIM THIS TIME!!

OKAY BUSTER! WHERE'S YOUR BILL FOR THAT CAT TIME LAST FALL?

SOON I GET IT TO YOU! MY WIFE SHE WRITE IT!!

NOT GOOD ENOUGH ARNIE! YOU AIN'T LEAVING THIS BAR 'TIL I PAY YOU AND A ROUND FOR YOUR TABLE!

OKAY! OKAY! YOU REAL TOUGH GUY MARTEN!

91-18

NO WONDER SOUTHERNERS CAN'T COMPETE WITH CUT-THROAT NORTHERN BUSINESS MEN!!

133

138

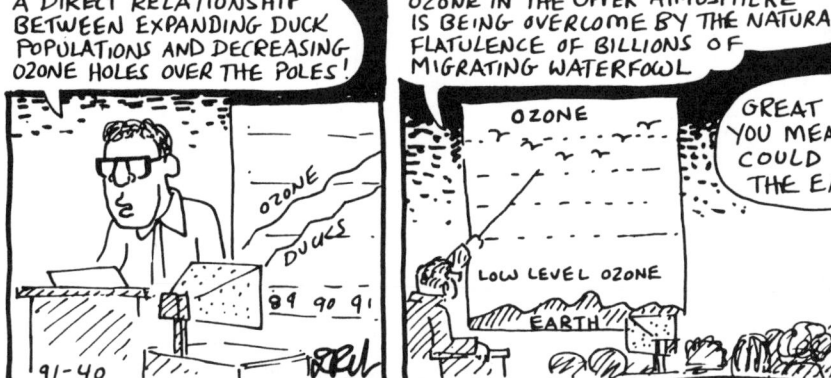

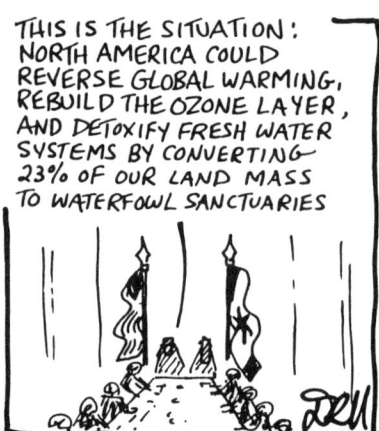

THIS IS THE SITUATION: NORTH AMERICA COULD REVERSE GLOBAL WARMING, REBUILD THE OZONE LAYER, AND DETOXIFY FRESH WATER SYSTEMS BY CONVERTING 23% OF OUR LAND MASS TO WATERFOWL SANCTUARIES

THIS WOULD DESTROY OUR RAPE AND PILLAGE GROWTH ECONOMY AND PUT OUR STANDARD OF LIVING ON A PAR WITH YUGOSLAVIA...

91-41

AS POLITICIANS WE HAVE A DUTY TO APPEAR TO BE DOING SOMETHING WHILE MAINTAINING THE INDUSTRIAL STATUS QUO...

EXCUSE ME SIR!! I THINK I'VE GOT THE ANSWER!!!

CONTINUED...

MR. BUSH, MR. MULRONEY I'VE FOUND A BIOLOGIST CONSULTANT FOR INDUSTRY WHO WILL REFUTE THE DUCK SALVATION HYPOTHESIS!

HE'S ALREADY TESTIFIED THAT CARIBOU THRIVE ON OIL DEVELOPMENT AND HE CAN TWIST ANY DATA TO MAKE BLACK SEEM WHITE!

CARIBOU LOVE PIPELINES!

91-42

DUE TO THE SCIENTIFIC DEBATE OVER THE VALIDITY OF THE DUCK SALVATION HYPOTHESIS, CANADA AND THE U.S. TODAY ANNOUNCED A FIFTY-YEAR JOINT RESEARCH AGENDA PLUS A 75 MAN JOINT COMMISSION WHICH WILL REPORT IN 2050. MEANWHILE THE DUCK REDUCTION PROGRAMS WILL CONTINUE!

CNN

THE END

91-43

YEAH! I MOVED BACK TO THE BUSH!

PILTDOWN IS THAT YOU?

IT'S CRAZY OUT THERE MAN! ONE DAY I HAD 3 BILLION DUCK EGGS ON THE FUTURES MARKET AND THE NEXT DAY I GOT WIPED OUT!!

HOW COME?

EVERY NORTHERNER WANTS TO TRY IT ON THE OUTSIDE...

LOOK ME UP WHEN THE MOOSE SEASON OPENS!!

BUT THEY ALWAYS COME HOME IN THE END!!

146

148

155

156

WOW! MARTEN! A WORLD RECORD FOR SURE!!

YEP! OVER 30 YEARS OLD! BEEN HERE EVER SINCE YOU WERE JUST A KID AND NOW YOU BOTH GOT KIDS OF YOUR OWN!

THIRD TIME THIS SUMMER OL' BUDDY!

93-34

NOW MARTEN THIS SUMMER PLACE HAS TO KEEP US IN TOUCH WITH NATURE!

TO FEEL THE WIND, SMELL THE FLOWERS, HEAR THE BIRDS, WATCH THE MOOSE... BE AT ONE WITH THE BUSH!!

93-35

BEST I COULD DO!!

I'LL JUST CACHE THE KEYS HERE

BUT I HAVE A SUPER VELCRO DOUBLE SNAP POCKET IN MY L.L. BEAN PANTS!

SURE! THEN WE GET MAULED BY A GRIZZLY WHO TEARS THE BUTT OUT OF YOUR FANCY PANTS! BROKEN AND BLEEDING WE CRAWL BACK TO THE TRUCK ONLY TO FIND WE HAVE NO KEYS!!!

HEY WHAT ARE YOU DOING?

CACHING MY WATCH MY RING, MY CREDIT CARDS, MY...

93-36

159

SKOOKUM'S RULES OF THE HUNT

1. THE MOOSE IS ALWAYS ON THE OTHER SIDE OF THE LAKE

OH NO!

2. WHEN YOU GET THERE IT'S A COW

OH NO!

3. JUST AS YOU'RE LEAVING THE BULL SHOWS UP

OH NO!

MY GRANDADDY HUNTED THIS LAKE WITH YOUR GREAT GREAT GREAT GRANDADDY!!

AND HE PROBABLY SHOT THIS MOOSE'S GREAT, GREAT, GREAT, GREAT GRANDADDY!

WHICH SHOWS THAT...

LIFE IN THE NORTH IS REALLY GREAT!!

SHAVE IT OFF!

WHAT?

EVERYTIME YOU COME BACK FROM HUNTING YOU HAVE HAIR ON YOUR FACE

AH BUT ZIS TIME I 'AVE ZEE MOUSTACHE OF A *LATIN LUVAIR*!!

OKAY YOU CAN KEEP IT... UNTIL *TOMMORROW*!!

"PAWS" creator: Doug Urquhart

For the past 30 years, "PAWS" creator Doug Urquhart has covered the north, working across Canada from Quebec to the Yukon as a prospector, biologist, game officer, weather observer, bush rat, jail guard, cartoonist, writer, and environmental consultant. For many years Doug had his own dog team which provided the original inspiration for "PAWS." Currently, he lives in Whitehorse, Yukon with his wife Judy and their children Robin and Kaitlyn.

"PAWS" celebrates the lifestyle of everyday people in small northern communities while at the same time poking fun at their idiosyncrasies. It also satirizes Northerners' efforts to cope with modern society in the form of tourists, bureaucrats and scientists as well as turning typical northern clichés back on the "outsiders" who invent them.

"PAWS" was created to counteract the overwhelming southern media by providing readers of small northern newspapers with humour about their own society rather than the standard fare of urban jokes from southern cartoon strips. Northerners often use "PAWS" to illustrate peculiarities of northern existence that cannot be expressed in any other way. Some regularly send strips to relatives in the south with the simple message, "This is why I live here!"

Index

A

addictions 35, 39

the Arctic 68, 69

B

the bar 48, 68, 69, 75, 81, 89, 90, 132, 149

bush tips 36, 38, 52, 57, 58, 65, 66, 79, 129

business 34, 39, 48, 76, 77, 116, 128, 132, 145, 156

C

city life 41, 54, 72, 74, 98, 108, 116, 135, 146, 147

D

dog's life 12, 16, 21, 22, 24, 25, 32, 40, 43, 53, 57, 61, 62, 66, 71, 75, 86, 87, 89, 91, 92, 95, 96, 98, 100, 101, 102, 103, 112, 115, 125, 126, 129, 144, 152, 160

E

the environment 26, 33, 62, 77, 78, 82, 85, 121, 124, 128, 134, 136, 137, 138, 139, 147, 148, 149, 150, 151, 152, 160, 163

explorers 17, 28, 29, 77, 114

F

fall 13, 83

fishing 6, 9, 10, 19, 46, 78, 127, 157, 159

flying 22, 23

G

government 12, 17, 25, 43, 49, 57, 63, 68, 70, 76, 79, 80, 99, 114, 126, 127, 133, 140, 143, 146, 151, 153, 155

grouse 24, 27, 163

guiding 17, 61, 86, 122, 128, 136, 158

H

health 30

hippies 15, 35, 36, 37, 88

horses 47, 122, 144

hunting 14, 31, 32, 46, 61, 67, 70, 72, 85, 86, 106, 107, 124, 127, 141, 151, 161, 162

K

kids 24, 30, 58, 59, 74, 123, 137

M

marriage 23, 33, 36, 49, 52, 56, 60, 66, 68, 71, 75, 76, 89, 90, 96, 97, 100, 102, 124, 141, 154, 157

mechanics 18, 66, 87, 145

money 32

mushing 1, 2, 3, 4, 5, 9, 10, 18, 20, 21, 34, 37, 43, 53, 55, 73, 74, 75, 89, 94, 98, 109, 112, 150

O

oldtimers 43, 93, 107, 126, 156, 158

P

philosophy 94, 102, 108, 109, 113, 115, 116, 121, 123, 130, 132, 134, 142, 144, 146, 152, 154, 155, 156, 157, 159, 161, 162, 164

police 11, 13, 27, 34, 44

politics 6, 44, 56, 67, 71, 73, 125, 139, 140, 142

prospecting 18, 29, 31, 64, 104, 123, 130

punks 16, 19, 47, 108, 130

R

ravens 21, 30, 47, 67, 71, 95, 104, 124, 134, 137, 138, 139, 140, 165

religion 7, 38, 45, 58

romance 4, 5, 16, 23, 35, 42, 50, 52, 55, 56, 71, 114, 145

S

scientists 11, 25, 28, 38, 63, 65, 67, 90, 120, 122, 127, 135, 137, 138, 139, 140, 150, 155, 163, 164

snowmachines 20, 149

southerners 49, 60, 62, 63, 72, 74, 76, 80, 81, 82, 99, 101, 103, 113, 120, 122, 131, 133, 136, 142, 146, 152, 153, 154, 158, 159, 160

summer 10, 27, 45, 64, 157

T

tourism 8, 21, 26, 33, 41, 44, 45, 46, 64, 80, 81, 83, 120, 125, 133, 135, 143, 158

tradition 84, 98

trapping 14, 19, 32, 56, 60, 72, 92, 94, 97, 107, 109, 112, 113, 128, 153, 165

W

weather 20, 50, 93, 101, 115

winter 50, 51, 107

Fine books from Lost Moose Publishing

Another Lost Whole Moose Catalogue, A Yukon Way of Knowledge, *by the Lost Moose Collective.*
"A compendious, eclectic, oversize, liberally-illustrated, off-the-wall, broadside of comment and advice on living out one's life in the Yukon" — *Books in Canada.*
More than 200 northerners contributed stories, facts, photos and tips on what life's really like in the Yukon. A great read. Everybody's essential northern book: a northern bestseller.
ISBN 0-9694612-0-8

The Original Lost Whole Moose Catalogue,
A Yukon Way of Knowledge, *by the Rock and Roll Moose Meat Collective.*
The classic. First published in 1979, this legendary compilation of information and anecdotes on life in the Yukon is back in print.
ISBN 0-9694612-1-6

Edge of the River, Heart of the City,
A History of the Whitehorse Waterfront, *by the Yukon Historical & Museums Association*
A loving and authoritative look back to the days of the busy waterfront in Whitehorse, where trains from the coast met sternwheelers from the Klondike at the foot of White Horse Rapids. Researched and written by Helene Dobrowolsky and Rob Ingram.
ISBN 0-9694612-2-4

Klondike Ho! *by Curtis Vos*
A cartooned history of the Klondike Gold Rush of 1896-98. Authentic, detailed, descriptive, with a touch of humour. Captures the whole mad rush in pictures and makes it easy for anyone to understand.
ISBN 0-9694612-4-0

Skookum's North *by Doug Urquhart*
A dog's-eye view of life in the north. A ten year collection of humour, warmth and insight in one great volume. Nearly 500 of the author's humorous "PAWS" comic strips published in newspapers across northern Canada and Alaska.
ISBN 0-9694612-3-2

Write to the following address for additional copies of this book, and for an up-to-date list of other books available from:

**Lost Moose Publishing
58 Kluane Crescent
Whitehorse, Yukon, Canada Y1A 3G7
Fax 403-668-6223
Phone 403-668-5076**